Original title:
Tales Beneath the Christmas Tree

Copyright © 2024 Creative Arts Management OÜ
All rights reserved.

Author: Juliana Wentworth
ISBN HARDBACK: 978-9916-94-124-9
ISBN PAPERBACK: 978-9916-94-125-6

A Journey Through Festive Eyes

In the corner lies a cat,
Wearing Santa's hat with style,
Plotting mischief with a grin,
As ornaments topple, oh what a trial!

Cookies left for Santa's fate,
But the dog took one for a bite,
Wagging tails in pure delight,
As kids laugh at this silly sight.

Snowflakes fall, a slippery guise,
As Grandpa tries to dance in cheer,
With every twirl, a little surprise,
The couch may just be his new frontier!

Presents wrapp'd with bows so grand,
Unraveled by hands swift and spry,
Yet last year's gift remains unplanned,
A fruitcake, oh my, oh my!

The Glint of Joyful Respite

Under the tree, a treasure trove,
Tinsel tangled in Dad's tight grip,
A toy train that won't behave,
As toddlers giggle and laugh at the slip.

Mismatched socks and fuzzy hats,
Grandma's knitting left in a lurch,
Yarn chasing cats in playful spats,
While everyone's eyeing the church.

The elf on a shelf, a naughty spy,
Hiding marshmallows, what a plight!
In the kitchen, Auntie's pie,
Mysteriously missing, out of sight!

With laughter echoing through the night,
Gifts unwrapped, such silly glee,
As grand illusions take their flight,
Magic lives in such comedy.

Beneath the Twinkling Canopy

Beneath the stars, a curious scene,
Mom's new recipe turns out so wry,
The turkey's strut, a little obscene,
While kids all giggle, a merry sigh!

Each light that flickers tells a tale,
Of socks mistaken for festive flair,
As cousins chase with giggles so frail,
A game of chaos fills the air.

Hats pulled tight and scarves a twist,
Snowmen built in a bumbling arcade,
But wait! Is that on your list?
A strange creation, a snowy charade!

The tree now a jungle of cheer,
Strings of laughter light the room,
Reliving memories, year after year,
In this merry, curious bloom.

Glittering Hopes in Silent Nights

Cookies on the table, crumbs on the floor,
Elves in the kitchen, trying to score.
Milk in the fridge, who drank it all?
Reindeer are dancing, heed the midnight call.

Stockings are hung, but one has a hole,
A cat with a mission, with mischief in soul.
Presents all jumbled, what chaos we see,
A puzzle for breakfast, oh, what could it be?

Moments Frozen in Time

Snowmen with hats, lost their heads in a fight,
Children are laughing, oh what a sight!
Sleds flying past, who's making that sound?
Oops, that was Dad, stuck in the mound!

Hot cocoa spills, marshmallows on the floor,
"Who made that mess?" Dad shouts out once more.
Wrapping paper wars, a colorful spree,
A gift box for Fido, not quite what we see.

Glimmers of Holiday Mirage

Tinsel on the tree, a glittering mess,
A dog in the corner, pretending to guess.
Lights that flicker, dance in the air,
Who tangled the cords? Was it the bear?

Gingerbread houses, they crumble and fall,
Frosting is missing, where did it crawl?
A surprise in the oven, smoke fills the room,
Was that a dessert or a kitchen to doom?

Under the Starry Embrace

Starry-eyed wishes, all sparkle and glow,
Santa in traffic, oh no, what a show!
Reindeer on break, munching on snacks,
Their little hooves tapping, no time for flacks.

Wreaths that are crooked, hanging with flair,
A raccoon caught snoozing, without a care.
Neighbors all giggling, with fruitcake in hand,
Hoping for laughter, the best kind of brand.

The Silence of Glimmering Dreams

Underneath the shining lights,
A cat tries to catch a twinkle,
Swatting at the ornaments,
Oh, what a curious sprinkle.

Uncle Joe has fallen asleep,
With a napkin on his face,
While a gift beneath him wiggles,
He dreams of a joyful race.

The cookies disappear so fast,
Leaving crumbs all on the floor,
Santa's on a sugar high,
Laughing, wanting just one more.

Mom's sweater is painfully bright,
It glimmers like a disco ball,
Dad wears socks that clash so hard,
We've crowned him the fashion churl.

Fragments of Wonder in the Air

A tiny elf on the mantle,
Winks at the curious crowd,
Hiding all the best secrets,
With laughter, oh so loud.

The dog steals a shiny gift,
With a bow upon his head,
Bouncing back like a kid in glee,
While our hearts are filled with dread.

Grandma tells her wild stories,
About a snowman with a hat,
Who danced on every rooftop,
Oh, what a merry spat!

The cocoa's thick and tasting sweet,
With marshmallows that float high,
While we sing with silly voices,
And let our worries fly.

The Frosty Tapestry of Time

Snowflakes fall like little laughs,
On every nose and cheek,
Kids are building snowmen tall,
While the older folks sneak peak.

A reindeer in a headlock,
By a boy who wears a grin,
As the snowball fight erupts,
We all rush to join in.

Presents with a little jig,
Dance around the room with glee,
The dog barks at the tape rolls,
A scene that's pure comedy.

With lights that twinkle above,
And laughter ringing clear,
We cherish every moment,
As memories draw near.

Hidden Wonders Near the Fire

By the fire, we gather round,
Hot cocoa swirling high,
A stray marshmallow takes a leap,
Oh my, how time does fly!

The stockings hang, but one has gone,
A mouse with grand ambition,
Dancing off with candy canes,
A true comedic mission.

Dad tries to crack some bad jokes,
But nobody's laughing loud,
Until the cat conks him on the head,
And curses the holiday crowd.

With secrets hidden in each box,
And mischief here and there,
This festive spot is full of laughs,
A joy we love to share.

The Magic Hidden in the Pine

Amidst the branches, lights aglow,
A kitten hid where nobody'd go.
With tinsel tangled in its tail,
It pounced on gifts without fail.

Ornaments danced, a jolly sight,
As grandpa snoozed, his snore took flight.
The cookies vanished, oh what a tease,
We found the crumbs but where's the cheese?

Echoes of Joyful Laughter

Uncle Joe cracked jokes so wide,
The punchline slipped, the guests all cried.
Squeals of giggles, soda sprayed,
A slip on ice, the plan mislaid.

With every joke, the room aflame,
A family circus, all play the game.
The howls of joy, a festive cheer,
Who knew that laughter filled the sphere?

Lost Letters to Santa

Little Timmy wrote a note,
With crayon scribbles, a careful quote.
'Dear Santa, please bring me a pet,
But where is my dog? Oh, I forget!'

Mom found it stuck in the old sock,
It lit up her face, the biggest shock.
She laughed so hard, she almost cried,
As Timmy shrugged, his heart open wide.

Stories Untold in Silver Snow

In the yard, snowballs took their aim,
As Frosty winked, we joined the game.
But oops! A face plant, what a chore,
Snowflakes danced, and we wanted more.

With mittens soggy, but smiles so bright,
We made a snowman that sparked delight.
'The carrot's missing, who snatched it fast?'
Turns out, it was eaten at last!

Echoes of Joy and Wonder

In a box, a cat took a nap,
Tangled lights like a froggy trap.
Grandma spilled her cocoa mix,
Oh, the taste! No kitchen tricks!

Gifts wrapped tight, but they can't hide,
A puppy chewed them, what a ride!
Laughter bursts like popping corn,
Stories shared of all things worn.

Ornaments of Heartfelt Lore

A treasure map drawn by a child,
With crayon doodles, oh so wild.
Hidden cookies near the tree,
Oops, they're gone; not meant for me!

A wooden soldier starts to dance,
In pajamas, we join the trance.
Each ornament tells a joke,
Like Uncle Joe, who sings and chokes!

The Magic at Midnight's Door

At midnight's hour, the fridge does hum,
Chocolate bars, oh boy, what fun!
With goofy grins, we sneak a bite,
Then tiptoe softly, avoiding fright.

The elf on the shelf plays peek-a-boo,
With candy canes all covered in goo.
Whispers of mischief fill the air,
While we dream of feasts, without a care.

Hushed Narratives of the Hearth

In cozy socks, we gather near,
With stories that bring so much cheer.
A snowman built with socks and hats,
Turned into a swamp of furry cats!

Giggles echo from room to room,
As we spot toys that go 'vroom'.
Tinsel drapes like a shiny beard,
While silly antics are revered!

Paths of Light Through Snowflakes

In the backyard, kids take flight,
Snowballs flying, pure delight,
Laughter echoes, cheeks aglow,
Frosty faces, moving slow.

A snowman stands, a silly sight,
Carrot nose, button eyes so bright,
He tips his hat, but not so strong,
And down he falls – what could go wrong?

The dog runs by, a blur of white,
Chasing shadows, oh what a fright,
He jumps and tumbles, lands in snow,
With a howl, he's ready for another show.

Footprints crisscross, a dancing spree,
Who has the best moves? Not me, not me!
We race for cookies, hot cocoa in hand,
In a winter wonderland, oh, it's so grand!

A Tapestry of Cheer and Wonder

Ornaments dangle, what a mess,
A kitty cat thinks it's a dress,
She jumps and lands with a playful twirl,
Now the tree looks like a tilted whirl.

A ribbon gets tangled, oh what fun,
Wrapping presents? It's never done!
Tape sticks to fingers, bows fly away,
At this rate, gifts won't see the day!

Grandma's cookies, a scrumptious treat,
But the dogs know where they meet,
Sneaky snouts, with a cheeky grin,
They gobble it down, both dog and kin.

Ho ho ho, the laughter rings,
As each silly mishap joyfully clings,
This merry chaos, a charming view,
In a tapestry of cheers, old and new.

Beneath the Wrapping Paper Lies

Under the layers, what could it be?
Is it a sweater, or maybe a bee?
Paper crumples, excitement grows,
All the guesses, oh how it flows!

A box of socks? A funny old shoe?
Mysteries wrapped, just waiting for you,
Kids are hunting for secret clues,
Amidst the giggles, a cat's snooze.

The paper flies in a wild flurry,
Everyone laughs, but there's a hurry,
To see what's hidden, treasure of fun,
Oh, let's unwrap before we're done!

Finally, laughter fills the space,
As someone finds a funny face,
A gift of joy, what else to say?
In holiday cheer, we dance and play.

The Song of the Evergreen

In the still of night, the lights blink bright,
Underneath, the pets creep with fright,
A gnome winks, a squirrel does flee,
As strings of popcorn sway with glee.

Tinsel glimmers, a magpie's delight,
He lands on the branch, ready for flight,
A Christmas dance, he hops, he sways,
Every moment is filled with playful plays.

A chorus of joy, the jingle bells ring,
As laughter erupts from each little thing,
What a sight, a peculiar scene,
Around the tree, where we all convene.

So gather 'round, let laughter flow,
In a song of cheer, let your spirit glow,
For within these moments, so sweet and bold,
The memory of fun brings warmth in the cold!

Frosty Hopes and Holiday Songs

In the garden, snowmen dance,
Their carrot noses in a trance.
Snowballs fly, laughter fills the air,
With orange hats, they're quite a pair.

A squirrel steals a cookie or two,
While reindeer try on shoes too blue.
The frostbite's chill, a crazy game,
As hot cocoa spills – oh, what a shame!

Jingle bells stuck on the cat's tail,
She dashes fast, a furry gale.
Wrapped presents with bows gone awry,
While kids giggle, the dog looks shy.

Legends Adrift in the Snow

Legends whisper in frosty air,
Of elves who trip without a care.
Santa's sleigh gets stuck in the mud,
As his reindeer play in the crud.

A snowman dreams of summer sun,
Wishing he could go for a run.
While children build him a hat too tall,
That topples over – oh! Down he'll fall!

Hot chocolate spills on the new rug,
The cat sits smug, a cozy snug.
Mittens missing, a big fuss made,
While grandma chuckles, her knitting laid.

Series of Starlit Memories

Under stars that twinkle bright,
We share our snacks in pure delight.
Fairy lights tangled in the trees,
As everyone laughs and swats at bees.

A gingerbread house leans to the side,
As frosting fumbles in holiday pride.
The tree's a wonder, ornaments stray,
And grandpa claims he jigs all day.

Snowflakes dance as we start to sing,
With off-key notes that laughter brings.
Frosted toes from the chilly ground,
In funny socks, our joy is found.

Echoes of The Season's Charm

Echoes ring from the kitchen bright,
As cookies bake, a sugary sight.
But Auntie's secret, she'll never share,
The recipe's lost in a snow-filled air.

Plates stacked high, they topple down,
With giggles erupting, all over town.
The dog rushes in for a crumb or two,
While kids dream of games in the blue.

Wrapping paper flies like confetti,
Each gift a surprise that's never quite ready.
Smiles and jokes bursting at the seams,
In the warmth of laughter, we chase our dreams.

Illuminating Shadows in the Pines

Underneath the branches wide,
A cat and elf in playful stride.
With candy canes, they wage a war,
And tinsel flies from every drawer.

A dog in hat, a goofy grin,
Chasing lights, it zooms right in.
While laughter bubbles, friends collide,
They trip on blankets, giggles glide.

The snowman winks with buttons bright,
As snowflakes dance in golden light.
Through muffled laughter, tales arise,
Of secret gifts and grand surprise.

With every joke, the night unfolds,
In laughter's grip, new legends hold.
Beneath the pines, in festive cheer,
The silliest moments draw us near.

Stories Interlaced with Light

The lights, they twinkle, oh so bright,
While Grandpa tells of Christmas night.
His stories twist, a humorous spin,
Of who stole cookies, cheeky grin.

Cousins giggle, hiding sweets,
While secrets pass in whispered feats.
The ornaments dance, a merry sound,
As chaos reigns all 'round the ground.

The stockings bulge with odd delight,
Like Auntie's cat that loves to bite.
With every chuckle, memories weave,
A tapestry of joy we cleave.

In this circus of fun and cheer,
The tales expand with each good beer.
With lights a-glow, and hearts so light,
We find our joy in every bite.

Memories Decorated with Laughter

In the living room, a scene unfolds,
With stories stitched in laughter bold.
The puppy chewed a gift-wrapped shoe,
As Dad proclaimed, 'Oh, what to do?'

With mistletoe above their heads,
Uncle stumbled, fell on beds.
A burst of cheer took over space,
With giggly hugs, a warm embrace.

The cookies baked, a burnt delight,
Yet everyone took a joyful bite.
And Grandma's yarn, a tangled mess,
Is laughed at still, we must confess.

With every gift that's wrapped with care,
Comes joyful bliss and playful flair.
In moments bright, our hearts do sing,
Of laughter's joy that Christmas brings.

The Refrain of Magical Moments

As snowflakes swirl like fairy dust,
A funny reindeer grins, we trust.
It dances round the Christmas tree,
In hilarious arcs, oh can you see?

The tree's adorned with socks and spoons,
As family hums their silly tunes.
While mismatched hats and laughs collide,
The magic flows, we take the ride.

With jingle bells that jangle loud,
And relatives at their goofy proud.
We share our tales, with laughter spry,
In every grin and every sigh.

So raise a toast to silly glee,
As we unwrap our history.
For every laugh, a moment bright,
In the chorus of this festive night.

Whispers of Winter's Glow

Snowflakes dance like scattered confetti,
Children giggle, their cheeks all sweaty.
The dog wears a hat, a sight to see,
Chasing his tail and barking with glee.

Hot cocoa spills, a marshmallow fight,
Santa's lost sleigh in the backyard sight.
Elves try to help, but one took a nap,
As we unwrap gifts and share a laugh.

Secrets Wrapped in Ribbon

Presents piled high, a mountain of cheer,
Guess what's inside? Oh, let's not be clear!
A cat in the box, a dog steals the wrap,
"Oh no!" we all cry, as we share quite a flap.

Grandma's new sweater, oh what a delight,
It fits the cat snug—what a funny sight!
Laughter erupts, as the chaos unfolds,
In the whirlwind of wrapping, our joy turns to gold.

Beneath the Evergreen Canopy

Beneath the green branches, secrets abound,
A squirrel in the tree makes a comical sound.
The ornaments dance, and the lights start to twirl,
As Uncle Bob trips, giving us all a whirl.

Mittens mismatched, socks on the floor,
The dog stole the turkey, oh what a chore!
With giggles and snorts, we share in the fun,
Underneath the bright stars, our laughter's begun.

Embers of Holiday Dreams

The fire crackles with stories untold,
Mismatched Christmas sweaters, bright and bold.
Dad's dad jokes ring out, oh what a joy,
As the kids roll their eyes at the old silly boy.

Grandpa's snoring still fills the night air,
While we sneak in some cookies we dared to share.
With giggles galore, we find our delight,
In the embers of dreams on this magical night.

Beneath the Starlit Boughs

Under branches, gifts abound,
With reindeer snacks left unbound.
A cat jumps up, with stealth so sly,
Knocking ornaments as they fly.

Uncle Fred can't find his shoes,
He wore them both — what a ruse!
The lights twinkle and dance with glee,
While Grandma snores beneath the tree.

The Gift of Fragrant Pine

The scent of needles fills the air,
Mom's burning cookies, too much to bear.
A mysterious knock at the door,
It's Aunt Edna, with her pet dinosaur!

The star is crooked, calls for repair,
As laughter echoes, we swim in cheer.
Cousins wrestling for the last bite,
Who knew fruitcake could start a fight?

Mirth in the Heart of Winter

In winter's chill, we gather round,
With cocoa spills upon the ground.
Sister's prank: a fake snowman,
It melts too quick; oh, what a plan!

The carols sing of peace and grace,
But little Timmy's made a face.
He's stuck inside a Christmas hat,
And now he's known as "Hat Cat"!

Secrets of the Festive Night

At midnight's hour, all's not bright,
Dad dons a wig to spread delight.
With Santa jokes and funny cheer,
There's secret laughter, oh so near!

The dog sneaks in, a gleam of mischief,
He's snagged the turkey — what a rift!
A chase ensues, across the floor,
Who knew a feast could cause such roar?

Guardians of the Glittering Night

Santa's sleigh is stuck in flight,
Elves are giggling, what a sight!
Reindeer munch on cookies sweet,
While kids dream of snowy street.

Frosty wears a funny grin,
Snowflakes dance, let the fun begin!
Mistletoe hangs, a sneaky trap,
For cats and dogs to nap and nap.

Pinecones hide a silly sock,
Who needs gifts? Let's watch the clock!
Sparkles twirl in festive glee,
Hiding secrets just for me.

As bells jingle loud tonight,
Laughter fills the frosty light.
For every giggle, there's a twist,
In this wild December mist.

Memories Tucked in Twinkling Lights

Silly hats and strings so bright,
Deck the halls with pure delight!
Gifts wrapped tight with pesky bows,
Watch out for cat who likes to pose!

Grandpa sneezes at the tree,
Ornaments dance around with glee.
A mishap sends the snacks askew,
And Uncle Joe spills cider too!

Tinsel's tangled in the air,
Mom keeps muttering with a stare.
But laughter bubbles, fills the space,
As we bake and frolic in this place.

Memories shine in glitter's glow,
Floating stories as we go.
Each funny moment, wrapped so tight,
In our hearts, a joyful light.

Amidst the Shadows of December

Snowmen wobble, hats askew,
One fell over, oh what a view!
Kids slide down the icy slope,
With giggles wrapped in winter's hope.

Under blankets, stories told,
Of Christmas past, both new and old.
Grandma shares her secret pie,
While grandkids stare with wide-eyed sighs.

Lights flicker like they're on a dance,
Each color spins, a merry prance.
In shadows hiding, mischief waits,
As prankster kids rearrange the plates.

Stockings bulge with candies sweet,
But who will share their special treat?
Together we laugh, let's make a scene,
In this holiday, bright and green!

Enchanted Ornaments of Yore

Ornaments giggle on the tree,
Each with whispers, full of glee.
One claimed it's a royal square,
While another dances in mid-air!

Mice sneak nibbling on the shores,
Of sugar, spice, and glittered doors.
As family gathers, tales unfold,
In bizarre rhymes and laughter bold.

A cat named Jingle finds a spot,
Nestled in bows, he takes a lot.
Each cozy hug and silly cheer,
Makes our memories crystal clear.

As laughter echoes through the night,
And candles flicker soft and bright.
With all these moments, timeless, free,
We cherish what's under the tree.

Enchanted Splendor of the Night

Beneath the twinkling lights so bright,
A cat with claws joins in the fight.
Tinsel tangled all around,
A jumping dog makes quite the sound.

Cookies hidden well with care,
Elves spying snacks from their chair.
The tree now shakes with giggle and sway,
As ornaments tumble down to play.

Grandma's sweater, a sight to see,
In colors that could scare a bee.
With laughter echoing through the hall,
We celebrate both big and small.

A snowman wearing dad's old hat,
Wobbles and wiggles; what of that?
In this season of merry cheer,
We share our joy, and shed a tear.

Vibrant Stories in Silent Snows

Upon the roof, what could it be?
A raccoon sipping Christmas tea!
With lights that blink in errant rhythm,
Our family giggles, far from wisdom.

The stockings hung with care, it's true,
Yet whose bright idea was the glue?
Now every gift sticks to the floor,
And every laugh rings out for more.

Snowflakes dance in wild delight,
As snowmen strike a comical fight.
The hot cocoa spills, oh what a sight,
As marshmallows take off in flight!

With jokes that tumble like the snow,
It's hard to tell where the laughter flows.
So gather 'round, enjoy the cheer,
For holiday warmth is finally here!

Whirling Dreams of Joyful Nights

The star atop is slightly bent,
A puppy chewed it, what a rent!
The gifts are wrapped with silly bows,
But find the socks? No one knows!

Santa's sleigh is parked askew,
While kids claim they still saw him too.
A game of hide and seek ensues,
With reindeer tucked in all the hues.

Grandpa's snoring like a bear,
While visions of sugarplums declare:
Don't eat the cookies left by the tree,
For they might just belong to me!

Giggles spill and hearts take flight,
On this enchanted, quirky night.
With every chuckle echoing bright,
Let's savor the joy until it's light!

The Sweetness of Holiday Echoes

Amidst the clutter of toys galore,
The cat claims victory on the floor.
With wrapping paper strewn about,
We burst with laughter, squeals, and shouts.

The kitchen smells of cookies baked,
But who will eat what grandma faked?
Each batch a mystery, what's the taste?
A chocolate chip, or something misplaced?

Lights flicker like they're taking turns,
While grandma's dancing, your stomach churns.
We cheer her on with smiles so wide,
"Keep those moves; just take it in stride!"

Then as we gather round the fire,
With tales of nutty shenanigans dire.
Radiant joy is our festive prize,
In holiday echoes, love never dies.

Legends Weaved in Sugar and Spice

A gingerbread man ran from the cat,
With frosting shoes on, how clever is that!
He slipped on a doll and flew up high,
Landed in cocoa, oh my, oh my!

The reindeer stole cookies, so bold and brave,
While elves giggled softly, mischief to pave.
A snowman with a carrot nose did a dance,
Forgetting the cold, he took quite a chance.

A pine cone served as a jester that day,
Telling funny stories in a humorous way.
Disguised as a gift, he caused such a scene,
When unwrapped, the laughter was fit for a queen.

So raise up your mugs, let's cheer and delight,
For tales spun with laughter make spirits feel right.
With each little chuckle, let joy fill the air,
In this season of laughter, there's love everywhere!

The Gift of Distant Memories

A vintage postcard from '93,
Showing Grandma's sweater and her pet flea.
Itched and scratched with a twinkling eye,
Laughed 'til we cried, oh how time does fly!

Remember the Christmas with socks as our flair?
We wrapped up the cat, gave him a scare!
He leaped through the room, knocked the tree down,
While we roared with laughter, lost in the sound.

The carols we sang, off-key and loud,
Outshine the gifts wrapped up in a crowd.
For every silly stanza, each giggling glimpse,
Is the magic of memories that makes our hearts blimp.

So unwrap each moment and hold them up tight,
For in those sweet chuckles, there's pure, shining light.
The joy is the present, no matter the past,
As we cherish our laughter, may it always last!

Whispers from the Frost-Kissed Past

The snowflakes fell with a whispering cheer,
Recalling the antics from yesteryear.
With snowmen that danced and twirled in the street,
Wearing mismatched boots, oh, what a treat!

Baking went wild when the flour did fly,
Fluffy snow clouds rose up to the sky.
The cookies were crooked, but smiles were sweet,
'Cause laughter was baking in every warm treat.

The fire crackled in a sassy reply,
As marshmallows jumped thinking they could fly.
A candy cane brawl with sticky delight,
Wrapped us in giggles that lasted all night.

So let's hoist a toast to the silly and fun,
For holidays bright as a fresh morning sun.
May the whispers of joy fill our hearts and our minds,
As we wink at the frosty, who knows what we'll find!

Stories Strung Like Lights

With lights on the tree that flicker and glow,
Come gather around for the tales we all know.
The one with the penguin who stole all the pies,
And escaped through the rooftops, what a grand surprise!

The garland that giggled, oh what a sound,
It rolled off the mantel and tumbled down bound.
Causing the cat to leap high in the air,
Knocking down tinsel with style and flair.

The stockings all filled with oddments, how grand,
A mix of old toys and nuts from the stand.
Each gift held a secret, a chuckle or tale,
Of times when our laughter would surely prevail.

So let's string our stories like lights on the tree,
And share all the joy, let it set our hearts free.
For in every twinkle, and every cheer,
Is the magic of laughter, let's spread it this year!

Secrets of the Glowing Night

In shadows deep, the secrets sneer,
Old Mr. Squirrel sips holiday cheer.
He hides his stash in a cozy nook,
But it's all just peanuts, not a single book!

The twinkling lights, a mischievous show,
The cat pounces hard, thinking it's snow.
But it's just a yarn, a crafty delight,
And the dog gives a bark, what a silly sight!

Gingerbread men dance under the tree,
But one lost his leg, oh dear me!
With icing for shoes, he hops all around,
Leaving crumbs everywhere, what a mess on the ground!

When midnight strikes, the giggles begin,
Santa's caught dancing, let the fun spin!
He trips on a gift, oh what a clatter,
But laughter erupts, who cares about the matter?

Hibernating Dreams of Festive Ages

Bears in their caves are still full of glee,
Dreaming of snowflakes and warm cups of tea.
But one bear awakes, oh no, what a fright,
He's missed all the feasting, it's even in sight!

Instead, he finds tinsel stuck in his fur,
With a chuckle he says, 'Oh what a blur!'
He munches on cookies, feeling quite grand,
Thinking he's king of this sugary land.

Elves in a huddle, planning their tricks,
Swapping the toys for some silly old kicks.
With a wink and a nod, they raise up the fun,
Tossing in glitter, oh what a run!

As everyone gathers for moments to share,
The bear stumbles in, but he's lost from his lair.
With laughter and joy, the party ignites,
In hibernating dreams, they found winter nights!

Reflection in the Season's Embrace

The mirror on the wall shows a jolly old face,
With a hat that's askew, he's lost all his grace.
Wipe the smudge off your cheek, what a silly sight,
'Twas just a piece of pie from last night's delight!

Stockings hung low, with secrets inside,
What will they find? A surprise or a ride?
A banana, a sock, and a small rubber duck,
Just what we needed, oh what luck!

A reindeer attempts to fly from the floor,
But trips on the rug, and lands with a roar.
The giggles erupt, as joy fills the air,
With memories made, none of us a care.

In this season's embrace, we laugh and we play,
With every mishap, the light fades away.
So gather around for a snicker or two,
In reflections so bright, we find joy anew!

The Enchantment of December Whispers

Whispers of wonder dance through the night,
The snowflakes giggle in pure delight.
They tickle your nose as they flutter and fall,
Creating a scene that enchants us all.

Cookies and milk, what a splendid affair,
The reindeer complain, "No carrots to share?"
They nibble on treats meant for old Saint Nick,
While he chortles along, not missing a trick.

The tree starts to sway, can you believe your eyes?
With ornaments clinking, they join in the guise.
'Twill be a performance of dazzling flair,
As lights shimmer bright in a magical air.

So pull up a chair and join in the fun,
With laughter and joy, we'll shine like the sun.
In this world of enchantment, let spirits soar high,
For December's sweet whispers can't help but fly!

Tales of Aged Laughter and Love

The cat wore a hat, quite absurd,
It looked like a gnome, or something you heard.
The dog was in charge, in his shiny bow tie,
They danced around, as the family would sigh.

Grandma's fruitcake flew, oh what a sight!
It bounced off the wall, causing such fright.
We laughed till we cried, clutching our sides,
As Uncle Joe yelled, 'At least it still glides!'

A reindeer on skates, what a wacky affair,
With socks on his hooves, he slid everywhere.
The laughter erupted, like bubbles in stew,
As the ice underfoot cracked, we all just knew.

Amidst all the chaos, the gifts piled high,
A sock for the dog, and some cookies, oh my!
Yet the best was the laughter that rang through the night,
A treasure of joy that felt oh-so-right.

Murmurs of Yuletide Magic

Under the mistletoe, a kiss went askew,
Grandpa popped out, with his loud 'Boo-hoo!'
We giggled and snickered, hearts full of cheer,
As Auntie let out a cackle, then spilled her root beer.

Elves in the corner, counting their dough,
Who knew that they'd start a small snowball throw?
With snowflakes of laughter, on hapless Uncle Ned,
He ducked too late, now there's frosting on his head!

The lights on the tree began to unwind,
As Cousin Clyde whispered, 'What's wrong with your mind?'
They blinked in confusion, a festive charade,
A twinkling surprise, as the room was invaded.

With cookies all gone, and milk dripped away,
We swiped at some chips, who cares what they say?
The greatest of gifts, no prices can bring,
Are memories of laughter that make our hearts sing.

Canopy of Dreams and Delights

The dog in pajamas, he thought he was neat,
With bells on his collar, a true holiday feat.
The kids rolled in laughter, what a silly sight,
Chasing him round, what pure Christmas delight!

A buffet of gadgets, yet none did work right,
The wrapping paper monsters all joined in the fight.
As grandma declared, 'Let's share some old tales!'
The paper was eaten, you wouldn't believe scales!

Penguins on ice, with hot cocoa in hand,
Slipped and they tripped, it was simply unplanned.
The snowman yawned loud and fell with a thud,
We struggled to breathe through a giggle-filled flood.

In the midst of chaos, we gathered around,
With elf hats and laughter, our joy ever-bound.
The magic we shared as the day turned to night,
Was the spirit we hold, radiant and bright.

The Spark of Cherished Moments

A partridge flew in, wearing glasses too wide,
He squawked like a champion, incredible pride!
With every misstep, a chorus of glee,
They begged for retakes, but just let him be.

In the corner lurked Cousin Lou's wild cat,
Knocking down ornaments with a PLOP and a SPLAT!
The laughter erupted, the mood couldn't dim,
As the tree turned to 'art' with a fancy new rim.

The stocking was stuffed with a mix of delight,
With socks full of jellybeans, oh what a sight!
A cheery old elf squeezed in with a grin,
And left us all laughing, that's where joy must begin.

So here's to the giggles that float through the air,
To moments that spark and banish all care.
For laughter is treasure, the best gift of all,
With friends and with family, we carry the ball.

Journey Through a Snow-Draped Dream

A snowman danced in a top hat tight,
With carrots chatting 'til late at night.
The reindeer pranced on the roof with glee,
While Santa sipped cocoa beneath a tree.

The elves spilled sugar all over the floor,
As gingerbread men ran right out the door.
Candy canes twirled in a merry chase,
While snowflakes giggled, no time to waste.

In a sleigh ride filled with jolly tunes,
They flung snowballs at the unsuspecting moons.
"Hey! Watch it!" cried the moon with a laugh,
But oh, what fun on this frosty path.

So bundle up tight, let's not be late,
For laughter and joy are the best kind of fate.
With each snowy step, there's magic in sight,
As we journey through dreams on this funny night.

Whims of Frosted Time

With snowflakes swirling like a wild ballet,
The trees wore ornaments all out of play.
A squirrel was stealing my gingerbread snack,
I chased him around till I fell on my back.

The carolers crooned, no rhythm or rhyme,
Their notes bounced around like a jolly old chime.
A cat joined the chorus, a fluffball so grand,
While the dog just howled, claiming the land.

Gifts wrapped in paper of vibrant delight,
Play hide and seek in the soft candlelight.
The presents all giggled, "Don't look at me!"
Till one toppled over, oh what a spree!

The clock struck twelve with a jolliest chime,
As laughter echoed through frost-minted time.
So join in the fun, let your spirit be free,
In this whimsical world full of whimsy!

When Stars Align in December

The stars aligned like a showbiz crew,
While Rudolph was busy tying his shoe.
Elves practiced dances, slipped here and there,
Swapping their hats for a wild winter flair.

The mistletoe whispered, "Oh lend me a kiss!"
But the dog jumped in, ruining the bliss.
A snowball fight erupted, a frosty delight,
With giggles and shouts, what a silly sight!

Trees wore lights that twinkled with charm,
While cookies conspired to cause such a harm.
"Oh no!" cried the frosting, "I'll never survive!"
As everyone laughed, feeling so alive.

And when the stars blinked from way up on high,
They winked at the fun, as if to imply,
That joy fills the air, no reason to frown,
For laughter's the best gift when the sun goes down.

The Heartbeat of a Silent Night

On a night so silent, yet full of cheer,
Santa got stuck with a pie too near.
Cookies giggled as milk did a dance,
While the stockings plotted for a wild romance.

The fireplace crackled, it told a tall tale,
Of reindeer who flew with a flip and a sail.
They leapt through the rooftops, oh what a scene,
While the cats planned mischief, all cute and mean.

Snowflakes tickled the noses so bright,
While everyone gathered, snug and polite.
A jolly old song slipped out into the air,
As the laughs filled the room, free of all care.

In this silent night, oh what a delight,
Every heartbeat swayed with joy and light.
So bring on the giggles, let's all share the fun,
As we celebrate magic, 'til the night is done!

Fables of Frost and Family

A snowman danced in brand new shoes,
While Santa lost his favorite snooze.
The reindeer pranced in silly ways,
As kids threw snowballs, laughing, amazed.

A cat climbed up the Christmas tree,
Knocked down the star, all with glee.
Bells jingled as the chaos roared,
Mom's hot cocoa? It was savored and stored.

Grandpa told jokes that made no sense,
While wearing a hat far too immense.
The fire crackled with warmth so bright,
As we rolled on the floor, what a sight!

With cookies perched in sight so grand,
A cookie thief? Oh, was that planned?
We laughed until our sides did ache,
'Twas the best day we ever did make!

Luminescence in a Winter's Tale

The lights twinkled like stars gone wild,
Mom baked cookies, we acted like a child.
The Christmas tree shook, we were confused,
Who took the candy? Oh, we all mused!

A snowball fight broke out so fast,
Dodging and ducking, who would last?
Dad slipped and fell, what a show!
Our laughter echoed through the snow.

Plates of fudge stacked high on the floor,
Sister sneaked in, then sneaked out the door.
With chocolate smeared on her bright red cheek,
We stared and laughed as we began to speak.

In the glow of night, we huddled near,
Sharing all stories, spreading cheer.
With every giggle, and every sigh,
These moments, oh how they fly by!

Whispers of Winter's Glow

The cat found a gift, it was a delight,
Tangled in ribbons, oh what a sight.
A puppy squeaked with glee, what a cheer,
As it chased after toy trains, oh so near.

The snow outside fell softly down,
As Uncle Fred danced, oh what a clown.
While Grandma's fruitcake sat on the shelf,
We all laughed quietly, afraid for our health.

Here comes the turkey, what joy it brings,
But Auntie did drop it, oh how it stings!
The table turned into quite the feast,
With laughter and jokes, we were all at ease.

As the clock chimed, the fun wouldn't cease,
With stories that spun until we'd all crease.
With hearts warm and bright, our spirits soared high,
We reminisced funny tales, oh me, oh my!

Shadows of Festive Dreams

The lights flickered on our odd-shaped tree,
While little Timmy climbed high, oh so free.
He slipped and fell with a bounce and a thud,
Covered in baubles, oh what a flood!

A mystery prickled, what's under the wraps?
Grandpa snoozed as we heard little snaps.
Sister just giggled, her secret to keep,
While under the tree, the cat was asleep.

Cards stacked high became a tall tower,
Until they collapsed, oh what a sours!
We all burst out laughing till tears filled our eyes,
While Mom just sighed, 'They'll find a surprise.'

With laughter that echoed, we shared our glee,
In the warmth of the night, just you and me.
Each shadow danced with joy in our hearts,
In festive dreams, this magic never departs.

Trinkets of Memories Untold

Pinecones dressed up in tinsel bright,
A squirrel steals cookies right from sight.
The puppy chews on the gift wrap grand,
While grandma's knitting goes out of hand.

Beneath the tree lies a strange old shoe,
The kids think it's magic, who knew?
Uncle Joe wears a hat that's too tight,
We burst into giggles, what a sight!

Fables in a Frosted World

Frosty the snowman melts down in shame,
As kids throw snowballs, oh what a game!
Rudolph misplaced his gleaming red nose,
And now he's just a reindeer who knows.

Elf on a shelf starts to wiggle and dance,
He trips on his feet, gives a comic glance.
With laughter and joy, we all share a scream,
The holidays glow like a wild, funny dream.

Legacy of Yuletide Shadows

Grandpa's old stories have grown some new twists,
Like Santa's lost reindeer in foggy mists.
Cousins plot mayhem with glitter and glue,
While dad plays Santa and gets stuck in the flue.

The cat leaps high, grabs a bauble with glee,
Down comes the tree! Oh, not again, whee!
In the chaos, we find love that won't fade,
Amidst all the laughter, memories are made.

The Hearth's Cozy Chronicles

Hot cocoa spills, oh what a parade,
Marshmallows bobbing in sweet escapade.
A snowglobe treasures flurries of fun,
While mom makes a feast that weighs a ton.

With laughter and giggles, the night carries on,
As we unwrap presents 'til the first light of dawn.
Grandma's old jokes still tickle the air,
In this cozy corner, love's always there.

Glimpses of the Past's Warmth

A sweater knit with love was found,
But who would wear such colors, so profound?
It sparkles like a disco ball at night,
Reflecting every joke and silly fright.

Grandpa's stories from the days of yore,
Of snowball fights and fun galore,
He'd trip and tumble on the icy ground,
While laughter echoed all around.

A fish-shaped ornament, strange and bright,
Hung from the tree, oh what a sight!
Mom swears it's a family treasure fair,
But I think it's just an old backyard scare.

Each year we gather, that much is true,
To share our quirks, my dad's red glue,
For every present that's wrapped just right,
We unwrap the giggles throughout the night.

Beneath the Glimmering Boughs

Under strings of lights, the cat finds glee,
Knocking down ornaments, oh what a spree!
He's pounced on the tree skirt with such delight,
Turning the living room into a playful sight.

A rogue cookie tin spills with a clatter,
Dad yells, 'Watch it! You'll make us all fatter!'
With icing on our faces, we sit and munch,
An elegant feast dismissed for such a crunch.

With mismatched socks and holiday cheer,
We sing off-key—much to every ear.
Grandma winks, "It's the chaos we love,"
As we toast with hot cocoa, and glow from above.

Check the stockings for treats we might find,
A goofy surprise that's one of a kind.
From socks that don't match to candies galore,
We're grinning and giggling—who could ask for more?

The Lanterns' Soft Embrace

Lanterns sway gently, casting shadows bold,
Each flicker a story of laughter retold.
A cousin who dances, a brother who sings,
The night wraps us lightly in warm, silly things.

An elf on the shelf with a cheeky grin,
Plots mischievous schemes as the night wears thin.
He's taken the pickle, we're all in a chase,
While Mom tries to save some leftover space.

The star on top is a bit out of line,
Which only makes us laugh over hot spiced wine.
We're thankful for memories formed in the light,
Creating merriment that lasts through the night.

A dance-off is brewing, can you feel the heat?
With snowflakes outside, we find our own beat.
In jiggles and giggles we hold tight our place,
With families entwined in this comfy embrace.

Revelations in the Quiet Hours

As midnight creeps softly, the world's fast asleep,
We sneak in the kitchen, the secrets we keep.
Chocolate and cookies are up for a grind,
Oh, the belly aches we might leave behind!

The ornaments whisper of kindness and cheer,
Of frights from the past that still linger near.
Each echoing giggle from deep in the night,
Makes shadows feel warmer, and futures so bright.

A card with a doodle, Dad's old silly face,
Illustrates moments that time can't erase.
We gather our stories, weaving them right,
Sharing our laughter, a heartfelt delight.

In the warmth of the season, we pause to reflect,
On all of the mischief that life can inject.
The memories we nurture, like lights on the tree,
Fill our hearts with joy, and keep us all free.

Secrets Wrapped in Tinsel

A squirrel's scheme with shiny globes,
He mistook them for his winter robes.
With every leap, he gives a cheer,
'Tis the funniest sight, oh dear!

Grandma's fruitcake in a box,
Its weight? Enough to build a fox!
The dog gave it a cautious sniff,
Then ran away, what a funny myth!

The cat climbs high, a ninja so sly,
Dangles ornaments from the sky.
With a swish of tail, he gives a shake,
And down they come, oh what a quake!

A gift from Uncle, it's a mystery,
Wrapped in paper, a sight to see.
But could it be a pair of socks?
Oh hope not, that's full of knocks!

The Night's Enchanted Hues

Lights aglow, a disco ball,
They dance about, the great hall.
With every flicker, laughter bursts,
A chorus of giggles, a funny thirst.

The reindeer prance, they've lost the map,
They're circling the tree, it's quite a trap!
With candy canes as their guide,
They trip and tumble, oh what a ride!

Santa's hat, too big to wear,
It slips and slides, without a care.
A jolly jig, he swirls around,
With giggles echoing, oh what a sound!

Frosty's nose, a candy treat,
He sneezes sprinkles, oh so sweet!
They stick to kids, like glue they cling,
A giggly mess, oh what joy they bring!

Beneath the Evergreen Canopy

Pine cones drop, a crunching sound,
What's this? A squirrel on the ground!
He hoards the snacks, a sneaky thief,
Taking Christmas cheer, oh what a belief!

The elf's slipped on the tinsel bright,
He spun around, oh what a sight!
With candy scattered, he gives a shout,
"Who needs a floor? Let's dance about!"

Back in the corner, gifts in a stack,
A cat's in there, hiding for a snack.
With a swat and a paw, he breaks the bow,
Oh silly kitty, what a show!

Hats exchanged in a funny game,
Whose is whose? No one can claim!
With laughter ringing, we all agree,
Christmas is best beneath the tree!

Stories Lurking in Frost

Outside the window, snowflakes twirl,
A snowman winks, oh what a whirl!
He tips his hat, a playful jest,
"Join me for fun, it's for the best!"

Elves at work, with mischief glee,
They stack up gifts just to see
Who would sneak and take a peek,
Giggles burst; it's hide-and-seek!

Mittens lost in the festive rush,
Finders keepers, oh what a hush!
A mitten fight, snowballs they fling,
The laughter echoes, as carolers sing!

And underneath, a pet does snooze,
Dreaming of cookies, with chocolate ooze.
When morning comes, what sights to see,
Oh funny moments set us free!

Glistening Hopes and Wishes

A snowy night, and Dad's lost the keys,
He laughs and shivers, pretending to freeze.
The dog steals the ham, what a sight to see,
Mom's shrieks of panic dance on the breeze.

Sparkling lights twinkle on branches so dear,
Cousin Tim's antics bring everyone cheer.
Grandma says, "Whiskers, please stay off the pie!"
But with a wink, he takes another sly bite.

The kids start to giggle; their giggles ignite,
As mistletoe hangs, causing playful delight.
Uncle Fred's epic snore crashes the feast,
But as we all chuckle, the joy is unleashed.

Through laughter and chaos, the night unfolds fast,
With memories woven, each moment will last.
We spread Christmas magic, we dance and we sing,
In this glad celebration, it's all a wild fling!

The Legacy of Frosted Wishes

Presents stacked high with no space for socks,
Uncle Joe wraps his gift with the dog's old box.
A label that reads, 'To you from your pup,'
We all burst in laughter, as we fill our cups.

The snowmen are squished, thanks to little feet,
Sister's grand plan is to take 'em out neat.
But snowballs go flying, and soon they're all wet,
The battle for warmth, oh, how could we forget!

Cookies half-eaten, they're crumbs on the floor,
Mom claims they're not real, but we beg her for more.
With milk in a pitcher and smiles from the heart,
Who knew that this evening would be such a start?

As carols erupt, there's a joyful reprise,
With glances exchanged, we all laugh till we cry.
The magic of laughter, it weaves and it sways,
In this frosty wonder, our hearts softly blaze.

Adventures in the Crisp Evening Air

Out in the cold, we bundle and race,
Snowflakes a-falling, we're lost in the chase.
Dad's nose turns bright red, he slips on a hill,
We can't help but cackle, and oh what a thrill!

The sleds zooming past, with shouts and delight,
Little brother trips on his scarf in mid-flight.
He lands with a thump, oh, such a grand sight,
We roll in the snow, laugh till the night.

With cocoa in hand, we share all our dreams,
Each wish comes alive in the flickering beams.
The fire roars softly, our fingers turn warm,
Yet chaos continues, that's part of the charm!

As stories explode in the crackling glow,
Adventures for years that we still don't quite know.
With giggles and sparks, our joy knows no bounds,
In keeping this magic, pure laughter resounds.

Chronicles of Yuletide Cheer

The cat on the tree, what a sight to behold,
Swiping at baubles, so cheeky and bold.
A crash and a tumble, oh goodness, oh my,
We're gasping for air, trying not to cry!

Rugrats in pajamas, with candy cane dreams,
Singing off-key, bursting at the seams.
A race for the fudge, who gets to the prize?
As sugar-filled laughter makes everyone rise.

Grandpa tells tales of his wild Christmas past,
We hang on his words, hope this night lasts.
With twinkling eyes, he shares mischief and love,
His chuckles ring out like a soft hand above.

Surrounded by chaos, we gather around,
From quirks to the giggles, joy knows no bounds.
In chronicles shared, we find warmth and light,
Our hearts filled with glee as we say our goodnight.

Flickers of Heartwarming Light

A cat in a scarf, oh what a sight,
He swipes at the ornaments, with all his might.
The tree shakes and quivers, it wobbles and tilts,
While we laugh in the chaos, our care fades, then wilts.

Gifts stacked in treasure, a mountain so grand,
Who knew wrapping paper could slip from your hand?
Uncle Joe's loud snores become quite the tune,
As we dance 'round the tree, under the light of the moon.

Glittery ribbons tangled around our knees,
We giggle together, while feasting on cheese.
A whisper of secrets that come to the fore,
As Grandma just finds her lost knitting once more.

With laughter, sweet memories fill up the room,
As the cat tries to pounce on the last bit of bloom.
Eggnog spills over, and we all share a grin,
In a flurry of joy, let the festivities begin!

The Hidden Gift of Tomorrow

A box with a bow, just sitting so still,
What's hidden inside? A dream or a thrill?
We shake it and rattle, oh what could it be?
A pair of loud socks, or weird shaped brie?

Grandpa grins wide, he knows just what's in,
From a hobby of fishing, a lure wrapped in tin.
He claims it's the best catch of all of his years,
While we hold back laughter, suppressing our cheers.

In the corner, the puppy digs under the tree,
With a passion and glee, just like you and me.
He finds something chewy and gives it a gnaw,
As he frolics and rolls, we can't help but guffaw.

The dawn brings more chaos, with gifts galore,
A mix-up with names, and we laugh even more.
As we gather 'round, let our stories abound,
With joy, fun, and laughter, our hearts are unbound!

Sheltered in the Essence of Winter

Snowflakes are falling, like dreams from the sky,
While we sit by the fire, let our worries all fly.
A mug full of cocoa, and marshmallows too,
As we giggle and share tales, our hearts feeling new.

Outside, the snowman has a crooked old grin,
With a carrot for a nose, and a hat made of tin.
The kids coat him grandly with all that they find,
Surprising his poise, leaving giggles behind.

Dancing in boots, we slip and we sway,
Spreading cold joy in the most clumsy way.
Wrapped in our scarves, we spin with delight,
As laughter rings out on this chilly, bright night.

With joy in our hearts, as we toss snowballs fast,
Warm memories created, let our laughter last.
For winter embraces, with fun and with cheer,
In this jolly old season, we find love, oh so near!

Threads of Whimsy and Cheer

The lights on the tree, they flicker and flash,
While Cousin Sue wraps her yarn with a splash.
"Look at my scarf!" she proudly exclaims,
But it's tangled in knots, and it's whole lot of flames!

The cookies are baking, a sweet pastry war,
Some misshapen snowmen, with icing galore.
"More sprinkles!" they shout, tossing some high,
While laughter erupts as they watch it all fly.

The dog chases shadows, he leaps with pure glee,
Spinning around, and he tramples the tree.
With laughter so loud, we forget all our woes,
In the dance of joy, creativity flows.

As we gather together, the joy is immense,
With bright happy faces, all jumping in suspense.
Forget the mishaps, let the blunders be dear,
For laughter is magic, a treasure to cheer!

Milton Keynes UK
Ingram Content Group UK Ltd.
UKHW021843151124
451262UK00014B/1283